KICKBOXING

Blocks, Parries, And Defensive Movement

From Initiation To Knockout

Everything You Need To Know (and more) To Master The Pain Game

by Martina Sprague

Copyright 2017 Martina Sprague

All rights reserved. No part of this book may be reproduced in any medium or form without the prior written permission of the author.

Other books of interest by Martina Sprague:

Formidable Fighter: The Complete Series

Fighting Science: The Laws of Physics for Martial Artists

Best Swordsman, Best Sword: Samurai vs. Medieval Knight

Knife Offense:
Knife Training Methods and Techniques for Martial Artists

Knife Defense:
Knife Training Methods and Techniques for Martial Artists

The Power Trip: How to Survive and Thrive in the Dojo

Lessons in the Art of War:
Martial Strategies for the Successful Fighter

TABLE OF CONTENTS

Introduction To Defense	5
Make Your Opponent Pay A Price	5
The Vicious Elbow	7
Body Mechanics For The Reverse Elbow Block	8
Exercises For The Reverse Elbow Block	10
In The Gym With Your Instructor	11
Body Mechanics For The Downward Elbow Block	12
Exercises For The Downward Elbow Block	14
Body Mechanics For The Inward Elbow Block	15
Exercises For The Inward Elbow Block	16
Recognizing The Openings	17
Forearm Blocks	20
Exercises For The Forearm Block	23
The Shoulder Block	26
Defending The Legs With Shin Blocks	27
Following Up Off The Shin Block	30
Generating Momentum Through Shin Blocks	34
In The Gym With Your Instructor	37
Exercises For The Shin Block	37

Leg Checks	40
Exercises For The Leg Check	42
Parries And Other Deflections	44
In The Gym With Your Instructor	45
The Pick And Counter And How Defense Triggers Offense	47
In The Gym With Your Instructor	49
The Trap And Redirect	50
In The Gym With Your Instructor	51
The Catch	53
Exercises For Parries	55
Defensive Movement—Slipping	56
Slipping Exercises	59
Defensive Movement—Bobbing And Weaving	62
Bobbing And Weaving Exercises	65
Guide To Concepts	69
Appendix	73
Preview: The Power Trip: How To Survive And Thrive In The Dojo	74

INTRODUCTION TO DEFENSE

Now that you have learned some offensive skills related to basic punching and kicking in other books of the *Kickboxing: From Initiation To Knockout* series, it's time to learn good defensive skills. A successful kickboxer must be complete in all aspects of his game, and offense cannot survive without defense, and vice versa. Defense can be broken down into three major target areas: lower body, upper body, and head. In addition, there are two parts to basic defense:

1. Blocks and parries.
2. Head and body movement.

Which part of your body you use (hand, forearm, elbow, shin) when blocking or parrying depends on the type of strike you are defending against and on your target. All blocks can be done with either the lead or rear hand (or leg). In addition, blocks can be either linear, as when meeting the strike straight, or circular, as when redirecting the path of the strike. Head and body movement can likewise be linear or circular and is determined by the type of strike you are defending against, and whether the movement is used defensively (slipping, bobbing and weaving, ducking), or offensively (jamming, gapping). As in the other books of the *Kickboxing: From Initiation To Knockout* series, all techniques are explained from a left fighting stance. If you are a **southpaw** (a left-handed kickboxer who fights from a right stance), you must reverse the descriptions.

MAKE YOUR OPPONENT PAY A PRICE

Many kickboxers think of defense as simply avoiding a strike or kick. But good defense has many other purposes. Your goal defensively is to make your opponent pay a price. The objective of good defense is four-fold:

1. **Protect you from harm.** If the defensive move fails to defend, it is of little value. A good block requires a minimum amount of movement with minimal target exposure. To accomplish this, block everything that comes above the waist with your hands, forearms, or elbows, and everything that comes below the waist with your legs. If

you get in the habit of dropping your hand to block a low kick, you will leave yourself open at the head. Blocks can therefore be broken down into upper and lower body blocks.

2. **Create offense.** Blocking, in itself, will not win the fight. It is impossible to protect against all strikes. You *will* get hit. You should therefore strive to use the momentum of good defense to launch a counterattack.

3. **Destroy your opponent's weapons.** Although the very nature of blocking is defensive, if you execute your blocks properly, they can be highly destructive to your opponent's offensive weapons. For the purpose of this training segment, you should change your mindset about blocking from defensive to offensive. Begin thinking of your blocks as strikes and not simply as means of thwarting your opponent's attack. By selecting the right block and executing it in the proper manner, we can punish our opponent's offensive weapons and eventually render those weapons harmless. Elbow blocks and shin blocks, especially, can be used to inflict enough harm on your opponent's strike or kick that he becomes reluctant to use it again.

4. **Tire your opponent.** It takes more energy to fight offensively than defensively. Defense, with its shorter and more compact moves, should therefore be used between offense to replenish your energies and tire your opponent. Superior defense, which encourages your opponent to throw lengthy combinations without landing anything of value, is likely to frustrate and tire him in seconds. In kickboxing competition, particularly when the fight may be lengthy, the person who tires first will likely lose. When your opponent is exhausted and frustrated, his defense is lacking. This is a good time to explode with offense.

We easily get in the habit of trading blows with our opponent. But since a single properly placed punch or kick can end the fight, you should fight with forethought and safety in mind. Being overly cautious, however, and trying to avoid every strike thrown at you will never win the fight. There is a fine line between offense and defense. While you should adopt an attitude of offense, you should also keep defense in the back of your mind and use it to feed your offensive techniques.

THE VICIOUS ELBOW

The elbow is one of the hardest bones in the human body and perhaps the most effective blocking weapon the kickboxer possesses. By using the elbows as weapons against your opponent's feet, shins, and fists, you can inflict damage to those offensive tools.

Using your elbows for blocking allows you to keep your hands high for protection. Avoid dropping your hand low to block, as seen here.

A properly executed elbow block against a kick can take away your opponent's fighting spirit, and may even crack his shin bone. We will explore the following three elbow blocks:

1. **Reverse** elbow block.
2. **Downward** elbow block.
3. **Inward** elbow block.

Although there are other types of elbow blocks, these three are quite effective as striking blocks. Let's look at the reverse elbow block first, which is designed to protect your ribs and kidney area, and is generally used to defend against the roundhouse kick. For more on kicking, see *Kickboxing: The Front Kick, Roundhouse Kick, And Side Thrust Kick*.

BODY MECHANICS FOR THE REVERSE ELBOW BLOCK

To execute the *reverse elbow block* against a roundhouse kick, bring your elbow an inch or two back and slightly down, driving it into your opponent's instep, ankle, or shin. For maximum effect, strike the target squarely with the point of the elbow. There is no need to drop the hand low, since a very short move is often sufficient.

Execute the reverse elbow block by jamming your elbow into your opponent's instep, ankle, or shin. The reverse elbow block is short and snappy and does not require much upper body movement. Return your hand to *point of origin* as soon as you have completed the block.

Pivot your body slightly in the direction of the block or in the opposite direction. Pivoting in the opposite direction may seem contradictory, but gives you more protection along your **centerline**. As your hand drops slightly with the block, tuck your chin down behind your shoulder. As a rule of thumb, and for maximum protection, pivot in the same manner as when throwing a strike. When blocking with your lead elbow, use the "jab pivot"; when blocking with your rear elbow, use the "rear cross pivot," as described in *Kickboxing: The Jab* and *Kickboxing: The Cross, Hook, And Uppercut*.

"Jab pivot" with reverse elbow block as defense against a roundhouse kick.

"Rear cross pivot" with reverse elbow block as defense against a roundhouse kick.

When pivoting your body with the block, transfer weight from one leg to the other to set for a follow-up strike. If choosing to pivot in the opposite direction as the block (jab pivot), blocking with your lead elbow sets you for a rear cross, rear hook, or rear uppercut. Blocking with your rear elbow sets you for a jab, lead hook, or lead uppercut. If choosing to pivot in the same direction as the block (rear cross pivot), the opposite is true, and you should now throw the counterstrike with the same hand that is blocking. Since most kickboxers drop their guard at least slightly when throwing the roundhouse kick, upon defending against this kick, try countering with a strike to your opponent's head.

EXERCISES FOR THE REVERSE ELBOW BLOCK

Let's work some exercises for the reverse elbow block. Have your partner whack your rib and kidney area with a focus mitt, while you work on blocking with the reverse elbow block. From a fighting stance with your guard high, drop your elbow straight back, as if you were elbowing somebody standing directly behind you. Drop your weight slightly with the block and return your hand to the high guard position as soon as the block is complete.

Now, move with your partner, and have him alternate left and right strikes to your rib and kidney area with the focus mitt. Observe your partner's upper body to determine from which side the strike is coming. Do not look at his hands. Relax your shoulders as much as possible, letting the reverse elbow block come naturally.

Next, have your partner wear shin guards while throwing roundhouse kicks to your rib area. Block the kicks using the reverse elbow block. Focus on blocking with the elbow and not with the forearm. Although the forearm will protect you against the kick, the elbow will inflict more damage. Practice throwing a counterstrike the moment your block impacts the target, preferably while your partner is still on one leg. The best time to strike your opponent is when he is in the process of kicking, because this is when his stance is potentially unstable and he is unable to move away. Try throwing a roundhouse kick to your partner's supporting leg, preferably to his inside thigh area, simultaneously blocking his roundhouse kick with your elbow.

Jam your elbow into your opponent's shin (first picture) and throw a counterstrike the moment your block impacts the target (second picture).

Since the roundhouse kick is effective from a variety of ranges, you can block a kick to your opponent's instep, ankle, or shin, depending on how far away he is when extending the kick. Have your partner throw roundhouse kicks from long range. Impact his instep with your elbow. Make sure he wears shin guards during practice sessions to decrease the risk of injury. Next, have him throw roundhouse kicks from short range. Impact his shin with your elbow.

Engage in light sparring with your partner throwing roundhouse kicks. Have him kick with **broken rhythm**, throwing multiple kick combinations and single kicks, pausing slightly between kicks. Practice using your peripheral vision to pick up on the movement of your partner's kicks. Use reverse elbow blocks to block as many kicks as possible, following each block with a counterstrike or kick.

IN THE GYM WITH YOUR INSTRUCTOR

Reverse elbow block! Drop your weight slightly with the block. This technique is great when throwing a follow-up strike off that same hand. When your opponent throws a roundhouse kick, he will likely drop his guard on that side and leave an opening at the head. I notice that you have a tendency to block with the muscle on your arm rather than with the point of the elbow. Blocking with the point of the elbow, and directing the block toward your opponent's shin or ankle, allows you to inflict maximum damage. Which way you pivot depends mostly on what kind of follow-up strike you have in mind. Are you setting for a rear hand strike or a lead hand strike, or for a kick?

Defend against the roundhouse kick with a reverse elbow block (first picture) and counter with a rear cross (second picture).

BODY MECHANICS FOR THE DOWNWARD ELBOW BLOCK

When your opponent has learned his lesson by getting his roundhouse kick blocked by your elbow, you can do the same to his front kick by using the *downward elbow block*. Most front kicks are thrown to the midsection. This bit of knowledge is helpful when it comes to defending against the kick. Since the groin and legs are illegal targets for the front kick, we know that the kick will go either to the body or head. The head is a difficult target to take successfully, because the kick must first pass the body on its way to the head. We can therefore say that all front kicks can be blocked as they reach our midsection. Never wait until the kick reaches head height to block it.

Execute the downward elbow block against a front kick by dropping your elbow straight down with the full force of your body behind it.

Impact your opponent's toes, instep, ankle, or shin with the point of your elbow. Return your hand to point of origin as soon as the block is complete.

When blocking a front kick with your elbow, tuck your chin down behind your shoulder for protection and drop your body weight slightly with the block. If your chin remains high, you will leave an opening for your opponent's counterattack.

Try the downward elbow block against a low jab. If your elbow impacts your opponent's fist or wrist, he will feel it through 14-ounce boxing gloves.

EXERCISES FOR THE DOWNWARD ELBOW BLOCK

Have your partner wear shin guards while throwing front kicks to your midsection. Block the kicks by dropping your elbow straight down along your centerline. Impact your partner's toes, instep, ankle, or shin. This takes a bit of precision, since both your elbow and your partner's foot are relatively narrow. Drop your weight slightly with the block. Each block should be short and quick with minimum movement in your arm and most of the power originating in your body. Return your hand to point of origin as soon as the block is complete in order to protect your openings.

Since the front kick is a long range technique (as opposed to the roundhouse kick, which works from both long and short range), a counterstrike may not prove effective. After blocking with a downward elbow, look for ways to step to a new angle closer to your opponent but off his *attack line*. What types of counterstrikes work best? Look for ways to counter-kick rather than strike following the downward elbow block.

After blocking a front kick with your elbow (first picture), step off the angle and throw a counterstrike from a superior position toward your opponent's back (second picture).

BODY MECHANICS FOR THE INWARD ELBOW BLOCK

The *inward elbow block* is a variation of the other elbow blocks that is used less frequently against a strike or kick to the midsection. It differs because your elbow does not drop straight down, but swings like a pendulum toward the centerline of your body. Use this block against a side thrust kick. Impact your opponent's toes or ankle rather than his heel, if possible, because these are more sensitive and prone to injury.

When using the inward elbow block against a side thrust kick, pivot your body off the attack line toward your opponent's centerline, and impact his toes or ankle rather than his heel.

The inward elbow block also works well when defending against punches at close quarter range. Use sharp and small moves when blocking punches to the body to avoid dropping your hand low. Use body movement instead of arm movement alone. Pivoting your body places more weight behind the block and increases its effectiveness. It also allows you to cover your ribs with your non-blocking arm.

Use the inward elbow block to redirect the path of an uppercut. The elbow should swing like a pendulum toward the centerline of your body.

EXERCISES FOR THE INWARD ELBOW BLOCK

Have your partner wear gloves while throwing straight strikes to your midsection. Block each strike with an inward elbow block. This block allows you to keep your hands high for protection. Execute the inward elbow block by keeping your fist stationary, allowing your elbow to swing like a pendulum toward your centerline. The movement should be short and snappy. The inward elbow block works best against a straight strike to your midsection, and is similar to a parry in that it redirects the path of the strike.

Whenever your opponent throws a straight strike to your midsection, he will automatically leave an opening at the head. After executing the inward elbow block, practice counterstriking to the opening. Try counterstriking with the hand on the same side as the block, and with the hand on the opposite side of the block. Which is quicker? Why? Now, try a counter-kick after you have completed the inward elbow block. For example, execute the inward elbow block against your partner's strike, then take a step back and throw a front kick to his gut.

Block a punch with an inward elbow block (first picture), and throw a front kick to the midsection or ribs (second picture).

RECOGNIZING THE OPENINGS

Get in front of a mirror and note the openings that occur when using large arm movements for blocking. Next, note how much better you stay protected when keeping your arms tight to your body and blocking by pivoting your body.

Think of every block as if it were a strike. Use the elbow block to protect you from harm and destroy your opponent's weapons by inflicting as much pain as possible. When your opponent throws a roundhouse kick, instead of taking the kick on the side of your arm, block it by dropping the point of your elbow into his ankle. When the pain starts to bother him to the extent that he stops kicking or becomes overcautious in his attempts to protect himself, move forward with explosive offense.

In addition from protecting you from harm, good defense thus creates offense. Every time your opponent throws a punch or kick, he automatically leaves an opening on himself. Your block is therefore an indication that an opening exists. Instead of *freezing* (tensing) when your opponent's strike hits your blocking arm or leg, retaliate with offense immediately. Practice *offensive defense* by learning to see the opening every time your opponent throws a strike, and by following that strike back and beating him to the punch. Where is the opening in the following pictures?

Kickboxing: Blocks, Parries, And Defensive Movement

Midsection/ribs and lead leg.

Supporting leg.

Ribs and lead leg.

Inside thigh and midsection.

Ribs, lead leg, and possibly chin.

FOREARM BLOCKS

Although the elbow is the most vicious blocking weapon, the forearms and shoulders can also be used against an upper body attack to protect you from harm. The movement of the forearm block is similar to that of the inward elbow block, but instead of swinging your elbow like a pendulum toward the target, your forearm should stay vertically straight. To increase the power, pivot your upper body in the direction of the block and impact your opponent's punch or kick with the "fleshy" part of your forearm.

Forearm blocks can be divided into *inward* and *outward*. The inward forearm block is used to block a strike that comes toward the centerline of your body (jab, rear cross, or front kick), and the outward forearm block is used to block a strike that comes toward the outside of your body (hook or roundhouse kick).

To execute the inward or outward forearm block, wait until your opponent's strike is almost at the target (don't reach for it). Then take a small step or pivot your body off the attack line, and deflect the strike with your forearm.

Use the inward forearm block (first picture) or outward forearm block (second picture) to defend against the roundhouse kick.

Note that although the reverse elbow block is one of the best blocks for defending against a roundhouse kick thrown to the body, many kickboxers tend to use the inward forearm block instead (blocking with the arm on the opposite side of the kick). This can prove dangerous, because it turns your body partly away from your opponent, exposing targets on your back and side of head. Your opponent can now throw the roundhouse kick a few times, then fake the kick to draw a block, and follow with a rear cross to your jaw.

In addition to blocking kicks, the inward forearm block can be used against a jab to the midsection. A good follow-up is the spinning back fist to the head. The slight rotation of your upper body in the direction of the block helps you set for the continued rotation of the spinning back fist. (More about spinning techniques in another book of the *Kickboxing: From Initiation To Knockout* series.)

Use the inward forearm block against a low jab (first picture), and follow with a spinning back fist (second picture).

There are also *double forearm blocks*. These are used much like the inward and outward forearm blocks but against stronger techniques that need extra reinforcement. To execute the double forearm block against a side thrust kick, evade the kick by pivoting your body off the attack line. Allow both of your forearms to impact the target simultaneously. This prevents the kick from going through your guard.

Impact your opponent's shin, using the sharp edges of your forearms (about one inch from the elbow). Note how the fighter has pivoted off the attack line, so that the side thrust kick passes in front of his body.

Now, try this exercise on forearm blocks: When your opponent kicks, your natural tendency is to step back and make the kick miss. But this places you in a disadvantaged position too far away to counterattack. Since regaining that distance is difficult, try stepping forward rather than back, and jam your opponent's kick with your forearms. You are now within striking range. As soon as you have completed the block, reset your body to point of origin and throw a counterstrike. In order for jamming to prove effective and safe, you must start your gap closure at the initiation of your opponent's kick and before it reaches maximum power.

EXERCISES FOR THE FOREARM BLOCK

Have your partner wear shin guards. Block his roundhouse kicks with inward forearm blocks. Use the forearm that is on the opposite side of his kick. If he kicks with his left leg, block with your left arm, and vice versa. When it comes to blocking kicks, the inward forearm block is effective primarily against a roundhouse kick, but can be used against a variety of midlevel and high attacks.

For greatest effect when using the inward forearm block, pivot your upper body with your forearm vertically straight and toward your centerline. Your forearm should impact your opponent's shin. Avoid blocking directly with the bone of the arm, or with the small bones in your wrist. The block is made stronger by turning your arm slightly, so that you absorb the impact on the fleshy part of your forearm. Although forearm blocks do not inflict as much damage as elbow blocks (since the forearm is bigger than the elbow with the power dispersed over a larger area), they are easier to use and do not require as much precision to execute.

You can also use the inward forearm block against a punch, but must now move your upper body slightly to the side to avoid getting hit. Practice the inward forearm block against your partner's jab. Impact his forearm with your forearm. Experiment with suitable follow-up strikes. How can you take advantage of the slight rotation the block has caused in your body?

The outward forearm block is used mostly to block a kick or hook to the head. Use it against your partner's roundhouse kicks by assuming a fighting stance with your guard held high. Bring your arm up by the side of your head, simultaneously tucking your chin down toward your chest for protection.

When fighting at close quarter range, expect hooks to your head. Practice the outward forearm block against your opponent's hooks. Keep your arm tight to your body. Leaving a gap between your arm and head risks getting your arm swatted into your head; raising your arm too high risks exposing your midsection.

Use the outward forearm block against your opponent's hooks to your head. Note how this fighter has failed to keep his arm tight to his body, exposing targets on his midsection and ribs

Engage in light contact sparring. Have your partner be the aggressor by throwing roundhouse kicks midlevel and high. Block kicks to the midsection with an inward forearm block and kicks to the head with an outward forearm block. When you get comfortable blocking, counter with a strike or kick.

Face your partner and start at one end of the room. Have him throw roundhouse kicks randomly, advancing with each kick. Practice the reverse elbow block and the inward forearm block in combination, and experiment with suitable follow-up strikes. The reverse elbow block will likely do more damage, while the inward forearm block is easier to use and prepares your body well for a counterstrike.

Reverse elbow block (first picture) and inward forearm block (second picture). Either block can be used as defense against a roundhouse kick.

Now, practice the double forearm block against your partner's roundhouse kicks. The double forearm block is stronger than the inward forearm block, due to the use of both arms. The disadvantage is that both your arms are tied up in the block, so counterstriking may be delayed slightly.

The double forearm block is a strong block that impacts your opponent's shin near the ankle and near the knee simultaneously. It works great against a high roundhouse kick.

THE SHOULDER BLOCK

A more unorthodox way to block punches is using your shoulder. The *shoulder block* is similar in motion to the reverse elbow block. As the punch comes toward you, rotate your body in the "jab pivot" with your weight transferring to your rear leg. Simultaneously tuck your chin down behind your lead shoulder. This increases the distance to your opponent. Take the punch on your lead shoulder. Your body is now chambered for a follow-up strike with your rear hand.

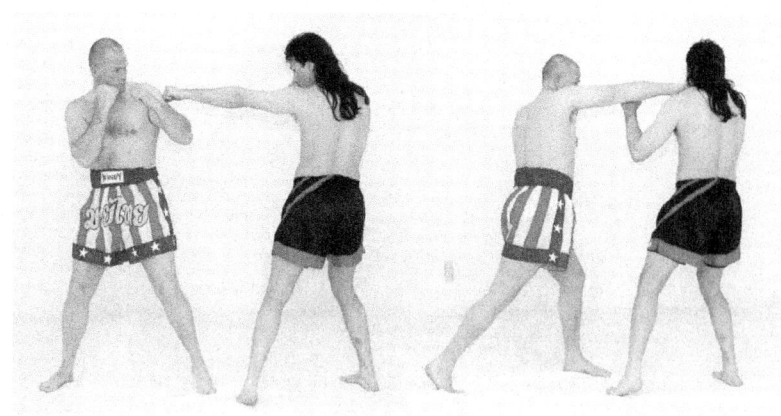

Block a punch with your lead shoulder going into the "jab pivot" (first picture). Counter with a rear cross (second picture).

Remember that you must be as committed to blocking as you are to striking and kicking. If you lack commitment, your opponent's strike will penetrate your block. If possible, your blocks should also inflict harm on your opponent's offensive weapons. The elbow block, due to the sharpness and hardness of the elbow, is one of the best blocks for defending and inflicting harm simultaneously. The elbow is very sharp and strong and has the ability to focus the power into a small area, inflicting great pain on the target. Using your elbow instead of your hand to block a strike or kick also allows you to keep your guard high and your arms close to your body for protection.

DEFENDING THE LEGS WITH SHIN BLOCKS

Since many kicks used in kickboxing are aimed at the legs, and since the legs are a fighter's support, it is crucial to learn how to defend against lower body attacks. Lower body blocks can be divided into:

1. Shin blocks.
2. Leg checks.

Shin blocks can be done with either leg. In general, your lead leg is faster than your rear leg since it is closer to your opponent. Shin blocks can be further classified as "outside" and "inside." The *outside shin block* is used to defend against an attack to your outside thigh area, which may be the most sought after target on the legs.

To execute the outside shin block with the lead leg, chamber your lower leg and point it at a forty-five degree angle toward line 1. Bring your knee all the way up to your elbow to ensure that there is no gap at your rib area. A skilled opponent will exploit any visible gap.

Meet your opponent's kick with the muscle on the outside of your shin and not with the shin bone, by extending your leg slightly outward and forward. This eliminates most of the power in his kick and reduces the risk of injury to your shin. It also helps you push your opponent off balance. Ideally, you should block your opponent's kick before it is fully extended.

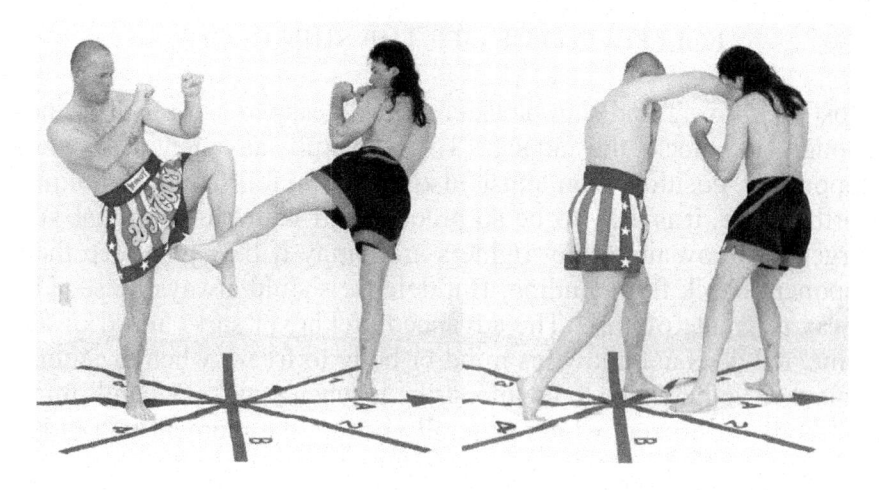

The *inside shin block* is used to defend against an attack to your inside thigh area. To execute the inside shin block, chamber your lower leg and point it in the direction of line 2. Bring your knee all the way up to your elbow.

While keeping your lower leg vertically straight, bring your shin forward and past your centerline, impacting your opponent's shin or ankle with the muscle slightly on the inside of your shin. When the block is complete, set your foot down and follow with a power strike, such as a rear cross or hook to your opponent's jaw.

As you can see, shin blocks allow you to defend against lower body attacks without a need to drop your hands. For greatest effect, the shin block should be executed at the initiation of your opponent's kick. As soon as you see the first twitch or movement in his hip, initiate the block and, if possible, step forward to jam his kick. This eliminates much of the power in his kick and places you at close quarter range, where you can follow with a punch combination. However, since it is not always possible to say whether your opponent's kick will come high or low, you may feel a need to raise your leg in the shin block motion even when the kick is intended for your body or head. Be aware of the danger associated with this move, as your opponent can take advantage of your positional weakness and attack your supporting leg.

FOLLOWING UP OFF THE SHIN BLOCK

Most kickboxers find shin blocks relatively easy to learn. But it's not enough to block the attack. To take full advantage of your opponent's position, you must also throw a follow-up technique. Furthermore, it is easy to be so preoccupied with blocking that you forget to follow up. Many fighters are happy if they just keep their opponent's kick from landing. But defense should always be seen as a way to create offense. The advanced kickboxer stays ahead of the game and does not allow his mind or body to freeze when executing a block. The best time to counterstrike is when your opponent's mind and body are frozen, which generally occurs the moment you block his strike or kick. The way your body is positioned after executing the shin block can determine your follow-up technique. Here are some possible follow-ups off the outside and inside shin blocks:

1. Block a roundhouse kick to your *lead outside thigh* with a lead outside shin block. Follow with a rear cross and a lead hook (shuffle forward as necessary). Since many fighters drop their guard when roundhouse kicking, an opening generally exists at the head. You can also follow with a roundhouse kick to the legs.

Use a lead outside shin block against your opponent's roundhouse kick prior to throwing a rear cross. Note how this sets your body for the strike.

2. Block a roundhouse kick to your *lead inside thigh* with a lead inside shin block. Follow with a lead leg side thrust kick (off the

same leg) to your opponent's gut. You can plant your foot before throwing the side thrust kick or come right off the shin block without setting your foot down first. Planting your foot between block and kick generates more power but is also slightly slower. Since the kick will likely knock your opponent back, you must follow with a technique that allows you to regain the distance (a stepping side thrust kick, for example).

Use a lead inside shin block prior to a side thrust kick. Note how this sets your body for the kick.

3. Block a roundhouse kick to your *rear outside thigh* with a rear outside shin block. Follow with a lead front push kick. Follow with additional strikes and kicks as distance increases. Alternatively, you can block the attack with a lead inside shin block.

Use a rear outside shin block prior to throwing a lead front push kick. Note how this sets your body for the kick.

4. The rear inside shin block is a bit more time consuming and might require a significant turn of your body, and is therefore not as practical. Block a roundhouse kick to your *rear inside thigh* with a rear inside shin block. Follow with a side thrust kick off the same leg. You have now switched stance.

Use a rear inside shin block prior to throwing a rear side thrust kick. Note how this sets your body for the kick. Note also how your rear leg effectively becomes your lead leg, assuming these fighters were in left fighting stances prior to blocking.

As previously noted, when shin blocking, bring your knee high enough to avoid leaving a gap between your knee and elbow. This forms a solid block along the entire side of your body, which can also be used as an effective upper body block against a side thrust kick. When your opponent kicks to your midsection, your block will impact the heel or bottom of his foot.

A good shin block forms a solid barrier and leaves no gap at your midsection (first picture). If you fail to raise your knee high enough (second picture), your opponent can land a kick to your ribs.

There is one more shin block worth mentioning, which can also be used as defense against a front kick or side thrust kick to your midsection. As the kick comes toward you, bring your lead leg straight up along your centerline and high in front of your body (same motion as if you were going to throw a front kick). Crouch forward slightly for protection and stability. Block the kick with your shin vertically straight in front of your centerline. Before your opponent's kick is fully extended, push off with your supporting foot to move your body forward and jam the kick. Note that this block requires a bit more precision than the previously mentioned shin blocks.

Use the straight shin block against a side thrust kick.

GENERATING MOMENTUM THROUGH SHIN BLOCKS

Once you get good at shin blocking and following up, look at using the momentum generated from replanting the blocking leg to help you launch a powerful kick with your other leg.

Execute a lead outside shin block (first picture). Set your foot back down and shuffle forward with a rear roundhouse kick to the front of your opponent's thighs (second picture). There should be no stop in momentum between the lead shin block and the rear roundhouse kick.

Execute a lead inside shin block (first picture). Bring the blocking leg back and replant your foot in position to throw a rear roundhouse kick to the back of your opponent's thigh or calf (second picture). The power of the kick is derived from the pivot in your body when bringing your blocking leg back.

Execute a lead outside shin block (first picture). Set your foot down and follow with a lead roundhouse kick to the back of your opponent's calf (second picture). As your foot plants on the floor between kicks, use the *tap and go* concept, reversing direction by allowing your foot to bounce off the floor.

Kickboxing: Blocks, Parries, And Defensive Movement

Execute a lead inside shin block (first picture). Set your foot down and follow with a lead roundhouse kick to the inside of your opponent's thigh (second picture). Again, rely on the tap and go concept. Keep the *beat* between kicks as short as possible.

Use the lead inside shin block as a setup for the spinning back kick. Since the inside shin block is slightly circular in motion, it can help you build momentum for a spinning technique, as seen in this picture sequence.

IN THE GYM WITH YOUR INSTRUCTOR

The inside shin block is a defensive move that can be used effectively as a setup for a side thrust or spinning back kick. Since the kick is likely to knock your opponent back, you must follow with a technique that allows you to regain distance: a stepping side thrust kick, for example. If this were in competition, where would your opponent be right now? On the ropes, right? So, unless you want to kick your opponent through the ropes and onto the judges' table with another side thrust kick, you must now work your way to the inside, or to close quarter range.

The side thrust kick is a good follow-up off the inside shin block and may knock your opponent' back. But once he is on the ropes, you must work your way to close quarter range.

EXERCISES FOR THE SHIN BLOCK

While elbow and forearm blocks are used to block attacks to your upper body, shin blocks are used to block attacks to your lower body. The primary advantage of the shin block is that it allows you to keep your hands high for protection. The shin block is executed by bringing your knee up to your elbow with your lower leg in the vertical position.

To develop effective shin blocks, start by toughening your shins on the heavy bag. Throw roundhouse kicks to the lower end of the bag where the filling has settled. Impact the bag with your shin. Since the shins are bony with very little padding, most people find even light contact to the shins uncomfortable. Try using light shin pads as a transition to harder contact. As you get used to the contact, increase the intensity or start kicking harder targets. Have your partner strike at your legs with a foam padded stick (lightly at first).

When blocking and countering a kick to your legs, the shin block is more effective when bringing the block slightly forward and into your opponent's kick. Start at one end of the room and alternate left and right shin blocks against an imaginary opponent, advancing forward with each block until you get to the other end of the room. Next, have your partner alternate left and right roundhouse kicks to your legs, advancing with each kick. Practice alternating shin blocks, inside and outside, stepping back each time your partner advances. Experiment with suitable follow-up kicks. First, counter-kick with the leg that is not blocking. Then, counter-kick with the leg that is blocking.

Work inside and outside shin blocks against your opponent's alternating roundhouse kicks.

When executing a shin block against your partner's kick, as your blocking leg lands, follow with a counterstrike to his midsection. If you can time the strike to land while your opponent is on one leg, you will likely knock him off balance.

Next, work the heavy bag, executing shin blocks against an imaginary opponent and countering with punches on the bag. Which types of follow-up strikes feel most natural? Identify the strikes that would most easily cause a knockout. When working the heavy bag, we tend to get into an offensive mindset and neglect defense. Make a conscious effort to incorporate blocks and movement into your bag work, even though the bag cannot strike you back.

Practice shin blocks against an imaginary opponent when working the heavy bag.

Finally, engage in light contact sparring with your partner. Practice shin blocks against roundhouse kicks thrown from close range with the shin rather than the instep. Block and follow with a short range punch combination (uppercuts and hooks). Step back to long range and have your partner occasionally fake a roundhouse kick. Note your reaction. Remember that you are vulnerable when on one leg. If your opponent fakes a kick that makes you raise your leg to block, he can take advantage of your position of weakness.

Fake a roundhouse kick to draw a reaction from your opponent (first picture). When he gets flustered or drops his guard, throw a rear cross to knock him out (second picture).

LEG CHECKS

The leg checks is a variation of the shin block and can be used to deter lower body attacks. The purpose of the leg check is to jam your opponent's kick, allowing you to get to close quarter range. The leg check requires speed and timing. When your opponent initiates a kick:

1. **Bring your lead leg up chambered and horizontal with the floor.** Your knee should point toward your centerline. For the leg check to prove effective, you must execute it at the initiation of your opponent's kick.

2. **Jam your opponent's kick** by dropping forward and into his upper thigh with your shin horizontal or diagonal across his leg.

Block a front kick or roundhouse kick with a leg check across the thigh.

As your opponent prepares to kick, place your shin across his middle thigh, disabling his ability to raise his leg. You can vary the technique by raising your leg as you close the distance to your opponent, creating a barrier against his kick. *Timing* is difficult to master, but well worth the practice. Once you develop the timing to catch his leg during its upward motion, your check will knock his kick back down, causing him frustration and pain to the middle thigh. When you use the leg check randomly, it tends to make your opponent hesitant to throw his kick, causing him to pay undue attention to the distraction and losing focus on his fight plan.

If your opponent is open at the ribs, you can also use the leg check as a strike against his body. When leg checking to the body, extend your hip at impact with the target to knock your opponent off balance. When the leg check is used against an attack to your legs, use your knee as the impact weapon. When the leg check is used to thwart your opponent's kick or knock him off balance, use the entire shin horizontally across his leg or body.

Kickboxing: Blocks, Parries, And Defensive Movement

Use the leg check against a kick (first picture) or against the body (second picture).

EXERCISES FOR THE LEG CHECK

Practice the leg check on the heavy bag. Your shin should impact at about midsection height horizontally across the bag. Use a shuffle-step (fast gap closure) prior to the leg check. Next, set the heavy bag swinging and time the leg check to the bag's forward momentum. If you can time the leg check to your opponent's forward motion, you will add his momentum to yours and stifle his attack.

Shadow box around the bag, then explode with a shuffle-step forward followed by a leg check to the midsection. As soon as your foot replants on the floor, follow with a punch combination. Move back to long range and repeat. Have your partner hold a kicking shield. Practice the leg check on the shield, using your forward momentum to knock your partner back.

Leg check the heavy bag and follow with a punch combination.

You can also leg check from close range by timing the leg check to the initiation of your opponent's kick. Your shin should come horizontally across his thigh. Explore suitable follow-up combinations, preferably a set of close range strikes. Also practice the leg check with your knee impacting the nerve center on the outside of your opponent's thigh.

Use your knee to check your opponent's outside thigh area. Impacting the nerve center can cause him considerable pain or a dysfunctional leg, similar in effect to a roundhouse kick to the outside thigh area.

PARRIES AND OTHER DEFLECTIONS

Now that we have talked about and spent some time practicing upper and lower body blocks, let's explore a variety of parries and defensive movement. The *parry* is an open handed deflection of your opponent's strike. The parry is not designed to block or stop an attack, but to redirect the path enough to make the strike miss. Since the parry is not a hard block, it requires very little energy.

Use the *inside parry* against a strike thrown to your facial area. To parry your opponent's jab with your lead hand, bring your hand at a forty-five degree angle forward from left to right toward line 2. Your hand should be open to the extent possible when wearing boxing gloves. Turn the palm of your hand at a forty-five degree angle forward, using the heel of your palm to deflect the strike. Stop when your hand gets in line with your rear shoulder. When you have completed the parry, bring your hand back to point of origin.

Since the parry is primarily a defensive move, your hand should only move enough to redirect the path of the strike. Keeping the parry short with minimal forward movement of your arm allows you to bring your hand back to point of origin quickly. Since the parry places your opponent in an inferior position with his centerline partly exposed or his back turned partly toward you, depending on whether you parry to the inside or outside of his arm, the parry is particularly beneficial when used in conjunction with a follow-up strike.

When parrying punches, start by looking for movement in your opponent's body. Do not look at his hands. Don't initiate the parry too soon (don't reach for the strike; let it come to you) or extend your hand beyond your shoulder, since this leaves unnecessary openings on your head and body. Decrease the risk of getting struck by your opponent's punch by pivoting your body off the attack line.

To parry your opponent's jab with your rear hand, as the punch comes toward you and just before impact, bring your rear hand at a forty-five degree angle forward from right to left toward line 1. Continue the parry past your face until your hand is in line with your lead shoulder to properly deflect the blow. When you have completed the parry, bring your hand back to point of origin.

IN THE GYM WITH YOUR INSTRUCTOR

Try counterstriking off the parry. Parry with your lead hand and counter with your rear. Parry a little closer to your opponent's wrist and not by his elbow. When counterstriking, aim directly for the target and not for your opponent's gloves. What are your targets? Jaw and nose. If you want to make his eyes water, go for the nose; if you want to take him out, aim for the jaw. Stay in a good defensive stance. Your hands are too close together and a little low. A good fighting stance places you out of reach of most of your opponent's counterstrikes. Have patience. If you rush in, you will get hit.

Parry your opponent's jab and counterstrike to the opening at his midsection.

Good defensive skills can be a life saver. When you get tired, rely on defense more than offense. You will not only get winded; you get arm weary, too. You'll get mentally fatigued. And when you're tired, you will get hit more. Good defense allows you to rest and replenish your energies. Good defense will tire your opponent. He will get frustrated and weary, and will eventually not be able to defend himself. And it will be like fighting a child.

When parrying your opponent's punch, you disturb his rhythm. Take advantage of it and exploit the gap at his chin or midsection.

THE PICK AND COUNTER AND HOW DEFENSE TRIGGERS OFFENSE

Once you have deflected your opponent's strike, you must take charge of the fight and turn defense into offense. Use the momentum of your defense to launch a counterattack. The effectiveness of a strike is determined by your ability to "set" for the strike and use your body weight for power. Another important element is your ability to throw the strike directly off a block. The *pick and counter* is a useful type of parry. When your opponent jabs, come over the top of his hand with your rear hand, cupping his hand in yours. This redirects the path of the strike downward and slightly away from your centerline. Before he has time to retrieve his punch, counter with a lead jab to the open target on his jaw. Your parrying hand should make a tiny circle down and back to the guard position.

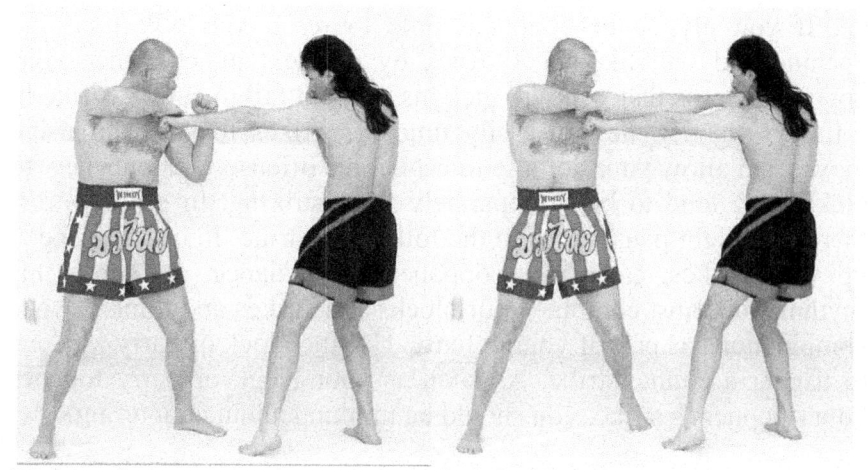

Pick and counter your opponent's jab. Note how both hands are used in unison. The moment your rear hand picks the jab (first picture), your lead hand starts forward to counterstrike (second picture).

When counterstriking, you can also draw the parrying hand slightly toward you and counter with a jab or rear cross off the same hand, or alternatively throw a strike off your other hand. In either case, your parry (or pick) and strike should happen at two different speeds. If the strike has the same beat as the parry, your opponent will already have withdrawn his hand to the guard position, and the opening will no longer exist. If he is quick, he may also strike with his free hand before your punch reaches him. Thus, to counter your opponent's strike effectively, your counterstrike must be faster than your parry.

Try this exercise on the pick and counter: Using proper footwork, move with your partner while he jabs at you randomly. Try to pick as many of his jabs as possible. Make sure that the distance between you and your partner is realistic, so that if your timing or accuracy is off, your partner's jabs will land. As you gain proficiency at picking, add a counterstrike with your lead hand. To make this more difficult, have your partner throw his jabs with broken rhythm, adding pauses between the jabs, and throwing doubles and triples in rapid succession.

Learning to pick your opponent's jab is not that difficult. The danger lies in becoming so concerned with defense that you fail to follow up. If you give your opponent time to reset, you will miss the opening and will likely get struck by his next punch. Once your opponent learns that you will pick his jabs but fail to counterstrike in a timely manner, he can easily time his strikes to your defensive moves and allow your defense to trigger his offense. Students new to kickboxing tend to block separately from striking. In other words, there is a slight pause prior to the follow-up strike. In order to speed up your strikes, catch your opponent off balance, and upset his rhythm, you must combine your blocks and strikes and think of your combinations as part of your defense. Use the block or parry as a cue to trigger a counterstrike. As soon as your block or parry touches your opponent's strike, you should be thinking about countering.

Try this exercise on countering in combinations: As you pick your opponent's jab with your rear hand, you gain momentum to throw a counter-jab with speed and power. This is part of the ***push-pull principle***, where the returning motion of your "picking" hand provides power for your striking hand. When your jab has landed and that hand starts on its way back to the guard position, your rear cross should be starting its motion forward. Your hands will make tiny circles on their return path, which allow them to complement one another. As one hand starts on its way back, it pulls and gives momentum to the other hand on its way out.

As you start the downward parry of your opponent's punch, you should also rotate your shoulders and body into alignment with your jabbing arm. This should be done in one simultaneous motion. Practice it slowly at first for proper technique. Then practice until the move becomes habit and can be done in a blinding flash. After your jab has landed, follow with another technique that feels natural to throw from that position. Each additional technique should be thrown without hesitation. Continue to build off the jab until you can throw three- and four-punch combinations with increasing speed, and without pausing between strikes.

IN THE GYM WITH YOUR INSTRUCTOR

As soon as you have parried or blocked a strike, you must follow with a good counterstrike to the opening you have created. Work on breaking your rhythm. Add more movement, or you will become predictable. Let's try something different today. Keep your hands open and slightly extended along your centerline. Use your hands to paw your opponent's punches away. Just circle your hands like this, and then transform the circling of your hands into a strike: either a jab or a rear cross. See how this builds momentum for your follow-up strike?

The open hand stance allows you to stay relaxed and interfere with your opponent's attempts to strike you.

A common error is failing to follow up off the parry. You parry and wait for your opponent's reaction. But by then it's too late. Also be aware that we often inadvertently raise our elbow with the rear cross or drop our rear hand below the chin every time we jab. To protect your openings, rest your elbow against your ribs. The moment your elbow falls behind your ribs, your hand will automatically drop low.

Keep your elbow in front of your body (first picture) When your elbow falls behind your body, your guard will drop low, exposing your head to blows (second picture).

THE TRAP AND REDIRECT

Some defensive techniques are a bit more difficult than others to use successfully and are generally not worked as often as the simple pick and counter. One such technique is the *trap and redirect*, which is designed to block your opponent's strike and also throw him off balance and open a target for a counterstrike. The technique is similar in concept to the pick and counter. The difference is that when you have picked your opponent's strike to the outside of his arm, you continue to circle your hand down and to the outside until your arm is nearly straight at the elbow, and your opponent's hand has been moved all the way off the attack line. This accomplishes two things:

From Initiation To Knockout: Everything You Need To Know

1. **It places you in a superior position** with your opponent's back turned partly toward you.

2. **It hinders your opponent's follow-up strike.** When his body has turned away from you, his strike lacks flexibility, reach, and power.

Trap and redirect your opponent's jab (first picture), and counter with a rear roundhouse kick to the back of his lead leg, which is now exposed (second picture). Note also the opening at the jaw.

You can gain proficiency with the trap and redirect by using it frequently in training. This increases your arsenal of techniques and allows you to defend yourself successfully against your opponent's strikes.

IN THE GYM WITH YOUR INSTRUCTOR

Have we talked about the trap and redirect yet, where you parry and hook your opponent's arm away from his body? Hooking your lead hand with my lead hand and parrying it down and to the outside, will open up targets on your jaw, ribs, and legs. It will also eliminate the threat of your rear hand. That's what I mean when I say that defense creates offense. Trapping and redirecting your rear hand with my lead hand, by contrast, will open up targets along the centerline of your body. Or if you throw a left-right combination, I can trap your lead hand first and then your rear hand, and then counter with a punch or a kick.

Try counterstriking with the same hand that is trapping. For instance, trap and redirect with your rear hand and make a tiny circle with your hand back to the point of origin. Then throw a rear cross, using the momentum from the trap and redirect. Or, conversely, trap and redirect with your lead hand and counterstrike with a jab.

Trap, redirect, and counter with the same hand.

Also try trapping and redirecting a kick, and countering with a kick to your opponent's inside thigh. Be aware that the trap and redirect drops your guard low for a moment.

THE CATCH

The *catch* differs from the parry in that it meets power with power. The catch can therefore be classified as a block. The catch is generally done with the rear hand for power, but can be done with either hand.

To catch your opponent's strike with your rear hand, start by bringing your hand forward at a forty-five degree angle toward line 1. Keep your palm open and facing your opponent. Extend your hand slightly forward along centerline A, and meet your opponent's strike before it is fully extended, stopping it in its track.

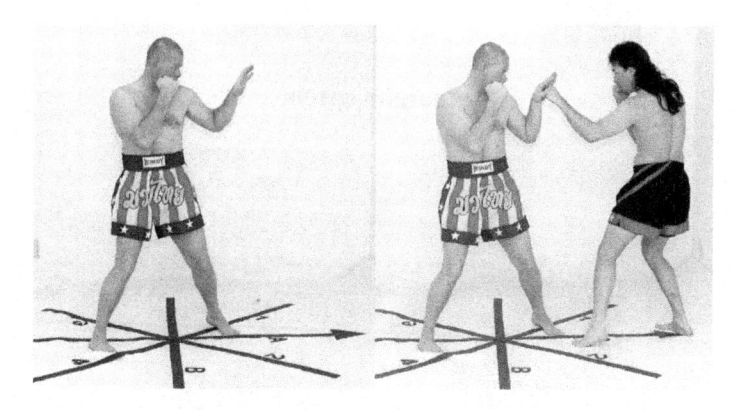

To catch your opponent's strike with your lead hand, start by bringing your hand forward at a forty-five degree angle toward line 2. Extend your hand forward along centerline A, meeting the strike and stopping it in its track.

The catch must be timed to impact your opponent's punch as your hand moves forward, meeting his momentum with yours. If your hand is stationary at impact, the force of your opponent's punch could swat your own hand back into your face. The beauty of the catch is that it hinders your opponent from throwing a counterstrike. If he tries to counter with a jab, for example, you simply execute the catch again. Since the catch meets power with power, it also has a tendency to knock him back, stalling his attempts to counterstrike.

A variation to the straight catch just discussed is the downward catch, which is used to defend against strikes that are thrown upward along the centerline of your body. The downward catch is the same in principle as the straight catch: Extend your hand to meet the power of your opponent's strike. Try it against an uppercut aimed for your chin.

Straight catch.

Downward catch.

Use fakes and deception to land strikes on an opponent who uses the parry or catch extensively. (More about this in another book of the *Kickboxing: From Initiation To Knockout series*.)

EXERCISES FOR PARRIES

The parry is a deflection of your opponent's strike. When your opponent is committed to a punch, he has momentum coming forward. When you parry his punch, the punch will pass over your shoulder. This places you at close quarter range. Since you have taken your opponent by surprise and his arm is still extended, he is open both at the midsection and head. This is a good time to launch a strong attack to his body. Parries are most effective against your opponent's weaker lead hand strikes (jabs), but can also be used against rear crosses. The pick and counter, trap and redirect, and catch are variations of the parry.

To parry and counter the jab, have your partner throw jabs at you from a left fighting stance. Use your rear hand parry to deflect the jabs. The parry is useful for getting your opponent's timing down. Once you get a feel for the rhythm of his jab, parry with your rear hand and immediately throw a jab. After each parry, bring your hand back to point of origin.

Repeat the exercise, but parry your opponent's jab with your lead hand. Once you get the timing down, follow with a rear cross. Countering with the opposite hand is more effective than countering with the same hand that parries. There are two reasons for this: First, your body is chambered for a counterstrike with the opposite hand. Second, it allows you to decrease the beat between parry and counterstrike. Now, move with your partner as he throws jabs at you. Vary the rhythm so that sometimes you simply parry his strike, and sometimes you parry and counterstrike.

Let's engage in some sparring practice using the parry. Parry your opponent's one-two combination (jab/rear cross), using your rear hand parry against the jab, and your lead hand parry against the rear cross. Throw a counterstrike after the second parry. If both you and your opponent are in left fighting stances, using your rear hand for parrying the jab is more beneficial, because the parry has a tendency to turn your opponent slightly to the side, giving you a superior position toward his back. Parrying with your lead hand, by contrast, places you in an inferior position in the path of his rear cross.

Parrying your opponent's jab with your rear hand turns his body to an inferior position with his back partly toward you, restricting the power and reach of his rear hand.

Engage in light contact sparring and work on parrying your partner's jabs and rear crosses, and counterstriking to different targets. Experiment with both low and high targets and countering with a kick rather than a strike.

DEFENSIVE MOVEMENT—SLIPPING

There are two ways to defend against an attack: You can block or parry, or you can use evasive movement. Using movement gives you the benefit of keeping your hands and legs free for counterstriking. When you move your head to the side to avoid a punch, it is called *slipping*. When you move your upper body side-to-side and below the path of a punch, it is called *bobbing and weaving* (or rolling). We will talk about slipping first.

Slipping (first picture) versus bobbing and weaving (second picture).

When fighting an opponent who favors long range techniques, moving from the outside to the inside (from long to short range) can prove tricky. You can jam your opponent's kicks to eliminate most of the power, but when fighting a good puncher you may need to rely on upper body movement to avoid his strikes. You must now learn to slip punches, duck jabs, and bob and weave underneath hooks.

The sideways movement of your head when you slip a punch allows the punch to pass over your shoulder. A slip generally precedes a bob and weave. Watch your opponent's upper body (shoulders in particular), and initiate the slip when you see the first movement of a punch.

Note how the weight shifts from one foot to the other when slipping. Keep one hand by the side of your head as a check, with the other hand ready to counterstrike.

Kickboxing: Blocks, Parries, And Defensive Movement

When slipping your opponent's punch successfully, there will automatically be an opening at his chin for your counterpunch. Be aware that some fighters jab a little more to one side than the other. Avoid slipping toward your opponent's punch. At the beginning of the round, feel your opponent out so that you know which side his jab is most likely to land on and avoid slipping to that side.

There is also a rearward slip, where you move your head back instead of to the side, increasing distance and making your opponent's punch short of reach. When slipping to the rear, be careful not to shift your weight to your rear leg, or your balance may suffer. Another danger occurs when your opponent throws a double jab. Once you have slipped his first jab to the rear and your head comes forward again, as it must in order for your body to correct itself, he can time his second jab to your head movement and add your momentum to his.

When slipping to the rear (first picture), be careful not to move into your opponent's double jab (second picture).

Try parrying in conjunction with slipping. For example, parry your opponent's jab to the inside of his arm with your lead hand, simultaneously slipping to the left. Or parry to the outside of his arm with your rear hand, simultaneously slipping to the right. If he throws a rear cross, the opposite is true. Throw a counterstrike immediately following the slip. Use very little separation between slip and counter. Think of it as "following your opponent's punch back in."

Parrying and slipping simultaneously gives you double protection.

SLIPPING EXERCISES

Many martial arts use rigid stances. The fighter's legs are rigid, his back is straight and rigid, his guard is still and rigid, and his head is rigid. Imagine that you are going to fire a rifle at a target. Is it easier to strike a stationary or a moving target? Since the head is such an attractive target in kickboxing (even if you were blessed with a real ugly mug), you should learn different ways to move the head in order to elude your opponent and make it difficult for him to land a strike. Once you have learned to make the head an elusive target through small and quick moves, look at how to move your whole upper body to evade a strike or kick. In general, upper body movement is most effective against a strike, but could on occasion be used to evade a head kick.

Let's practice slipping in front of a mirror. Place a two-inch wide piece of tape vertically down a mirror. Stand about one arm's length from the mirror, so that when you look at your reflection, the tape runs down the centerline of your body. Experiment with moving your head to the side in order to move it completely off the tape. The tape represents your opponent's punch.

Many fighters move their head excessively, using up energy needlessly. What other dangers are associated with too much head movement? Are you placing yourself in the path of yet another strike? Short head movements are faster than large head movements. When using short head movements, the strike might graze against the side of your head. But rather than hurting you, it may only stun you. With practice, you can learn not to let it bother you.

When practicing head and upper body movement in shadow boxing, make it as natural as possible, and part of your footwork, strikes, and kicks. We tend to think that it is necessary to move only when threatened by a strike. But continuous slipping is also beneficial when disguising strikes.

Upper body movement should be relaxed and without thought.

Now, have your partner glove up and throw punches at you. Keep your guard down and force yourself to use only head movement to avoid his strikes. Slip either left or right. Is there a time when it is better to slip left? Right? In general, moving your head to the "outside" (away from your opponent's centerline) is a little safer, because you won't be directly in his line of power. What benefits does slipping to the outside give you regarding your follow-up strike?

Slipping can also be incorporated simultaneous to blocking a strike. Have your partner throw punches at you. Keep your guard high and work on blocking or parrying the punches in conjunction with head movement. Your opponent's punch must penetrate your guard, and then find the target behind the guard. If the target (your head) is moving, your opponent's accuracy when punching decreases. Practice double slips to avoid two successive punches. Never assume that your opponent will throw only one strike.

Double slip two jabs, first to the outside away from your opponent's centerline as seen in the first picture, and then to the inside toward your opponent's centerline as seen in the second picture.

Which targets are best suited for your counterstrike? Can you counter-kick rather than punch? Have your partner throw strikes that you avoid with head and upper body movement. When the strikes miss, throw a counterstrike or kick. Ideally, you want to counter while your opponent's arm is still extended. Fights are not won through defense alone, however. When your opponent's strike misses, he will likely take another swing. Knowing this in advance gives you the opportunity to beat him to the punch.

Finally, work the double-end bag, incorporating slips with punches that set the bag swinging. First, throw a punch to set the bag in motion. When the bag comes toward you, move your head enough to make it miss, as if it were a punch thrown at you. When you start to master this, add a counterstrike to your head movement. Next, try slipping slightly to the rear instead of to the side. Time your head movement to the motion of the bag, so that when your head comes forward again, your "opponent" is in the process of withdrawing his strike.

DEFENSIVE MOVEMENT—BOBBING AND WEAVING

When fighting an opponent at short range, use bobbing and weaving instead of slipping. *Bobbing* is the vertical movement of your body, and *weaving* is the horizontal movement of your body. Good bobbing and weaving has four objectives:

1. **Avoid** getting hit.

2. **Confuse** your opponent.

3. **Set** your body for a counterstrike.

4. **Move from long range to short range** safely, so that you can follow with a hook or uppercut combination.

Bobbing and weaving is also referred to as *rolling*. Roll from your knees and not your waist, keeping your chin down and your eyes focused on your opponent. Stay visually aware of your targets and your opponent's actions. Keep your guard up to avoid getting hit with a hook to the head.

Note how the fighter shifts his weight from one foot to the other when initiating the bob and weave, and how he bends primarily at the knees when rolling under his opponent's hook.

If your opponent throws more than one strike, you risk getting hit when resetting from the bob and weave into your stance. You should therefore roll toward your opponent. Once you have closed the gap, your opponent must create distance to strike effectively. This leaves you in charge of the fight. When you are ready to move back to long range, do so while simultaneously keeping your opponent occupied with strikes or kicks.

Try this exercise on bobbing and weaving: Stretch a rope at shoulder-height from wall to wall across the room or ring. Start at one end bobbing and weaving under the rope until you arrive at the other end. Move the foot closest to the direction of travel first (concept: ***basic movement theory***), readjusting the width of your stance with your rear foot. Return to the other end by bobbing and weaving backwards. Bend at the knees and not the waist to keep your chin protected and your eyes on your opponent.

Work the same drill with broken rhythm. Take a couple of short steps between each bob and weave, or do a couple of quick rolls without stepping. Also add punch combinations in the air. For example, bob and weave from right to left under the rope and throw a lead hook followed by a rear cross. Then bob and weave back to the right and throw a rear cross followed by a jab or a lead hook if the distance seems right. Mix offense with defense. When you get to the end of the rope and your imaginary opponent has his back to the ropes of the ring, experiment with different ways to finish him.

Instead of waiting for your opponent to throw a punch that you can roll under, stay unpredictable by using a lot of upper body movement even when he doesn't throw a punch. When the punch comes, work the roll in with the rest of your movement. Also use broken rhythm when working your way to the inside. When it is time to move out, either roll out or jab out.

Some fighters avoid a punch by *ducking* it. You do this by lowering your body straight down by bending at the knees, keeping your back straight and letting the punch pass over your head. There is no sideways movement of your body or head when ducking.

Duck a punch by lowering your body straight down with your back straight.

BOBBING AND WEAVING EXERCISES

Let's start by practicing bobbing and weaving under a rope. String a rope about shoulder-height from one end of the room to the other (or have two students hold each end of the rope). Start at one end and bob and weave under the rope. Weave from left to right, then reverse and weave from right to left. Note how proper bobbing and weaving requires a lowering (ducking) of your upper body and head movement (slipping) underneath the rope. There should also be a slight sideways movement of your upper body.

Bobbing and weaving helps you avoid a strike that is thrown from the side and aimed at your head (hook, roundhouse kick, spinning heel kick, etc.) Each time you bob and weave under the rope, take a short step forward, starting with your lead foot and adjusting the width of your stance with your rear foot. Why is it important to stay in your stance and not step forward the way one would normally walk? Think basic movement theory. When you get to the other end of the rope, bob and weave backwards. When is it more beneficial to move forward versus back?

Bobbing and weaving is frequently done as defense against your opponent's hook. Have your partner throw hooks to your head. Avoid the strikes by bobbing and weaving under them. Is it better to weave toward or away from the punch? Why? Weaving toward the punch places you in the superior position toward your opponent's outside. When he misses with the punch, you will be positioned slightly toward his back. He must now readjust his stance before being able to strike you. If you weave in the same direction as the strike, you risk getting struck when coming back up in your stance.

Bobbing and weaving toward the hook (first picture) places you in the superior position toward your opponent's back (second picture), from where you can throw a counterstrike without risk of getting struck back (third picture).

Note how the bob and weave chambers (sets) your body for a follow-up strike. Which type of strike seems most natural to throw off the bob and weave? Which type of kick lends itself to your upper body movement? When your opponent throws a hook or roundhouse kick aimed at your head and misses, where does he leave himself open? Knowing in advance where the opening is helps you train for a logical follow-up technique.

Practice bobbing and weaving in shadow boxing. First, shadow box for one minute, using only defensive and evasive moves. Then, shadow box for one minute, adding counterpunches and kicks. Shadow boxing, using defense only, requires good visualization skills.

Now, mix up your movement in shadow boxing for variety. For example, bob and weave from left to right, and throw a punch that you are chambered for. Next, move around throwing punches and kicks. Next, visualize your opponent throwing hooks or roundhouse kicks at your head. Bob and weave under the attack and throw a counter-kick that you are chambered for. Next, do a couple of quick bob and weaves from left to right and back. Mixing it up teaches unpredictability.

Good partner practice further helps you refine your defensive movement skills. Have your partner throw a jab followed by a hook. Slip the jab by moving your head slightly to the side. Then, bob and weave under the hook. Use your peripheral vision to pick up on the movement of the hook. Ideally, you want to bob and weave in the opposite direction of the slip, because your head and upper body are already chambered for this. Since you cannot know with absolute certainty which strike your opponent will throw next, you must be ready to adapt. Should head and upper body movement be used when your opponent is not counterstriking? Why, or why not?

Counterstrikes can be practiced realistically on focus mitts held by a partner. Have your partner hold a focus mitt in one hand and wear a glove on the other hand. When he throws a hook with his gloved hand, bob and weave under it and counterstrike with power to the focus mitt, simulating a strike to his head. The idea is to make the bob and weave subconscious, where you implement offense automatically without having to think about your next move.

Now, try the double bob and weave. This simulates an evasive movement against two successive looping strikes: a left hook followed by a right hook, for example, or a left hook followed by a right roundhouse kick to the head. Why is it illogical to reverse the latter combination and have your partner throw a right roundhouse kick followed by a left hook? If your opponent misses with the roundhouse kick, he will not be in position to throw a left hook, because he will have his back turned partly toward you. If he

Kickboxing: Blocks, Parries, And Defensive Movement

initiates with the hook and misses, by contrast, he can use the miss to chamber for the roundhouse kick, with his feet already positioned for this move.

Now, practice bobbing and weaving with both high and low counterstrikes. Avoid being a headhunter. Start on the heavy bag. Bob and weave under an imaginary punch, and counter with a strike or kick to the midsection. Move around and throw some punches and kicks. Then bob and weave again and counter with a strike or kick to the head. Get with a partner in a light contact sparring match. Avoid his hooks by using upper body movement. Vary your counterstrikes to high and low targets.

Most kickboxers tend to favor offense over defense. Bobbing and weaving lends itself to offense since you can position for a counterstrike through the avoidance of your opponent's strike. You can also avoid a strike by moving back to long range, by taking a step back simultaneous to the bob and weave. If you counterstrike now, you are better off using your longer reaching legs. For example, bob and weave as you take a step to the rear, and counter with a front kick to your opponent's midsection. When your opponent misses with his strike and you have moved to long range, he will likely step forward and attempt to close the distance. If your timing is good, you can stop his forward movement with a front kick.

Bob and weave simultaneous to taking a step back (first picture), and counter with a front kick (second picture).

Can you throw a side thrust kick after moving to long range? How about a roundhouse kick? Why are the front kick and side thrust kick more beneficial than the roundhouse kick? Also try bobbing and weaving and counterstriking while in close, then moving out with a couple of quick straight strikes to your opponent's head. You are vulnerable when backing up, so it is especially important to throw strikes that keep your opponent occupied with defense.

Referee tending to a fallen fighter.

GUIDE TO CONCEPTS

ATTACK LINE: The attack line is created by linear movement between you and your opponent. When you move back in a straight line, it allows your opponent to attack more effectively. This linear attack can be thwarted by sidestepping or pivoting off the attack line, thereby forcing your opponent to adjust to the new position. By contrast, if you are the aggressor and your opponent is moving back in a straight line, you have the upper hand and should keep him on the attack line.

BASIC MOVEMENT THEORY: When moving, step with the foot closest to the direction of travel first, readjusting the width of your stance with your other foot. This helps you maintain balance by preventing you from crossing your feet.

BEAT: You can increase the speed of a combination by decreasing the beat between strikes. However, a short or steady beat is not always to your advantage. An irregular beat may benefit you more through the confusion it causes your opponent.

BROKEN RHYTHM: A steady rhythm can be used as a setup; however, it also has its drawbacks. Once your opponent gets in tune with your rhythm, he can cover his openings and block your strikes. To stay unpredictable, change your rhythm by speeding up or slowing down. A good way to learn broken rhythm is to count the beats in your head, speed up and slow down the count, and make your physical body do the same.

CENTERLINE: The centerline refers to an imaginary line approximately five inches wide, running vertically on the front and back of your body. Striking targets on the centerline can cause serious injury or death.

FREEZING: Freezing is the involuntary and often damaging tensing of muscles that happens when stunned or confronted with a threat. Freezing inhibits further muscle movement until you can relax. Making your opponent freeze is therefore a good tactic that allows you to take advantage of his moment of weakness. There are many ways to freeze your opponent's weapons. For example, a sudden, unexpected move will generally solicit a reaction that causes a defensive-minded opponent to freeze for a second. Touching any part of your opponent's body can also cause him to tense. Touching his gloves may cause his arms to freeze long enough that you can land a strike without being countered. However, you must also strive to eliminate your own tendency to freeze. Think like this: Every time your opponent lands a strike, whether to a valid target or just to your arm, use it as a cue to throw a counterstrike. In other words, use your opponent's offense to trigger your own offense.

OFFENSIVE DEFENSE: Defense is taken to a new level when you start using it offensively. An offensive move executed with good timing will interfere with your opponent's technique enough to keep it from landing. Likewise, a defensive move that simultaneously hurts your opponent (an elbow block to his shin, for example) will destroy his offensive weapons. The purpose of defense is therefore not merely to protect you from harm, but to make your opponent pay a price by destroying his offensive weapons and opening targets for your counterstrikes.

POINT OF ORIGIN: Wherever a technique leaves from, it must return to. There are mainly two reasons for this. First, in order to reset your body for a follow-up technique, your hand or foot must return to its original position. Second, any time you throw a strike or kick, you automatically create an opening on yourself. To minimize target exposure, it is imperative that you bring your "tools" back to the guard position.

SOUTHPAW: A southpaw is a fighter who fights from a non-conventional stance with his right foot forward. Generally, those who are left-handed fight from the southpaw stance, placing their left hand to the rear for power. It may benefit a right-handed fighter to develop the ability to switch to southpaw stance.

TAP AND GO: Planting your foot briefly between two successive kicks thrown with the same leg allows you to bounce your foot off of the floor, increasing the speed of the second kick. The tap and go concept also gives you better balance than when throwing the second kick without first planting your foot.

TIMING: Timing is the ability to take advantage of your opponent's targets, movement, or power by executing precise strikes, blocks, or movement when both of your positions are ideal.

APPENDIX

This appendix includes a preview of *The Power Trip: How to Survive and Thrive in the Dojo*, also by Martina Sprague.

PREVIEW

THE POWER TRIP:
HOW TO SURVIVE AND THRIVE IN THE DOJO

This is a preview of *The Power Trip: How to Survive and Thrive in the Dojo*, also by Martina Sprague. Many students have little knowledge of what to expect or how to increase motivation, retention, and rate of learning when first signing up to study the martial arts. You are left in the hands of an instructor who is often a student himself, not a teacher by profession, and who has little or no knowledge of the learning process or the psychology of teaching. As a result, the instructor simply states the facts—this is the name of the technique, and this is how it is done—without considering why the technique is done, the concepts behind it, and how to tailor it to fit your individual traits.

Learning the facts, or learning the mechanics of a technique, is the first stage of learning. But if you fail to go beyond rote memorization, you are unlikely to gain proficiency even in the simplest techniques. To understand this idea better, I like to use the analogy of the martial artist and the historian. The historian does not merely memorize battle dates and names of great generals. He or she studies with the intent of uncovering the underlying currents that shaped those events and learn from them. The same is true when learning the martial arts. Whether learning from a book or through hands-on experience, the underlying currents help you understand why a technique or concept is important. For example, a recent article about self-defense for the street stated, "No matter how scared you are, don't let your emotions show." The fact is, "Don't let your emotions show." While it is easy to agree with this statement, theoretical knowledge of the fact does not make you proficient at performing or understanding the technique. When confronted with life and death, just *how* do you learn not to let your emotions show?

As students of the martial arts, we often go to the training hall without considering exactly what we can do to further our learning. The glory is in performing our art and not in pondering the learning process. The purpose of *The Power Trip* is to educate you about the science of learning, instill confidence through familiarization with and recognition of a multitude of scenarios, and give you the power to act when you encounter specific problems. It is about making your education more profitable by showing you *why* rather than *what* to learn, and showing you how to teamwork with your instructor and peers even when your instructor and peers are uneducated about the learning process and cause you "problems." *The Power Trip* will give you the power to survive and thrive in the Dojo, by showing you how to recognize and counter situations when your instructor or peers are sitting on their "high horses" ready to go on a power trip that can prove to be more than a nuisance to you.

Furthermore, by looking at different situations from both the student's and instructor's viewpoint, you will learn about the many difficulties the instructor faces. The insights you gain will help you appreciate the instruction more and give you options for a mutually productive learning experience. You will learn how to turn a mediocre training session into an advantage, where everything your instructor and peers say and do is used for your gain.

As you continue deeper into your training remember that, although it is your instructor's responsibility to help you progress in the martial arts, it is equally much your responsibility to help your instructor pave the way for good learning to take place. I once overheard a conversation between two ladies discussing how much fun it was going back to college years after graduating from high school. One lady said that she didn't understand why the youngsters don't want to go to school, when you "just sit there and get spoon fed." But learning is a two-way street and often not as simple as taking in what is fed to you. Your instructor, no matter how talented, is only half of the learning process. Although you can't do much about your instructor's teaching methods, you do have considerable control over how you approach the lessons. *The Power Trip* will show you how to extract the information that your instructor and peers possess but don't necessarily know how to express, so that next time you go to class you can meet your instructor halfway and contribute with the missing half that makes the learning process whole.

It has been said that forewarned is forearmed. If you are a new student in the martial arts, ready to sign up for your first lesson, this study will give you a lot of information about the difficulties you can expect to encounter sometime throughout your training, and give you options for resolving potential conflicts. If you are a seasoned martial artist with years under your belt, you will no doubt recognize many of the scenarios presented, and be able to look back at your journey and consider what you could have done differently. This study will also arm you for the day you will begin teaching the martial arts (or help you improve your technique if you are already teaching) and show you how to build your integrity and repute as an instructor. Since the advice is not style specific but explores a multitude of scenarios that frequently play themselves out in the martial arts training hall, it applies to students of most martial styles.

About the author:

Martina Sprague has a Master of Arts degree in Military History from Norwich University in Vermont. She has studied a variety of combat arts since 1987. As an independent scholar, she writes primarily on subjects pertaining to military and general history, politics, and instructional books on the martial arts. Of interest might be her fourteen-booklet series titled, *Formidable Fighter*. For more information, please visit her website: www.modernfighter.com.

Other books of interest by Martina Sprague:

Formidable Fighter: The Complete Series

Fighting Science: The Laws of Physics for Martial Artists

Best Swordsman, Best Sword: Samurai vs. Medieval Knight

Knife Offense:
Knife Training Methods and Techniques for Martial Artists

Knife Defense:
Knife Training Methods and Techniques for Martial Artists

The Power Trip: How to Survive and Thrive in the Dojo

Lessons in the Art of War:
Martial Strategies for the Successful Fighter